SUGGESTIONS FOR GROUP LEADERS

1. **THE ROOM** Discourage people from sitting outside or behind the main circle – all need to be equally involved.

2. **HOSPITALITY** Tea or coffee on arrival can be helpful at the first meeting. Perhaps at the end too, to encourage people to talk informally. Some groups might be more ambitious, taking it in turns to bring a dessert to start the evening (even in Lent, hospitality is OK!) with coffee at the end.

3. **THE START** If group members don't know each other well, some kind of 'icebreaker' might be helpful. For example, you might invite people to share something quite secular (where they grew up, holidays, hobbies, etc.). Place a time limit on this exercise.

4. **PREPARING THE GROUP** Take the group into your confidence, e.g. 'I've never done this before', or 'I've led lots of groups and each one has contained surprises'. Sharing vulnerability is designed to encourage all members to see the success of the group as their responsibility. Ask those who know that they talk easily to ration their contributions, and encourage the reticent to speak at least once or twice – however briefly. Explain that there are no 'right' answers and that among friends it is fine to say things that you are not sure about – to express half-formed ideas. However, if individuals choose to say nothing, that's all right too.

5. **THE MATERIAL** Encourage members to read next time's session *before* the meeting. It helps enormously if each group member has their own personal copy of this booklet (so the price is reduced either when multiple copies are ordered or if you order online). *There is no need to consider all the questions.* A lively exchange of views is what matters, so be selective. You can always spread a session over two or more meetings if you run out of time!

   For some questions you might start with a few minutes' silence to make jottings. Or you might ask members to talk in sub-groups of two or three, before sharing with the whole group.

6. **PREPARATION** Decide beforehand whether to distribute (or ask people to bring) paper, pencils, hymn books, etc. If possible, ask people in advance to read a Bible passage or lead in prayer, so that they can prepare.

7. **TIMING** Try to start on time and make sure you stick fairly closely to your stated finishing time.

8. **USING THE CD/AUDIOTAPE** There is no 'right' way! Some groups will play the 14-minute piece at the beginning of the session. Other groups do things differently – perhaps playing it at the end, or playing 7/8 minutes at the beginning and the rest halfway through the meeting. The track markers (on the CD and shown in the Transcript) will help you find any question put to the participants very easily, including the Closing Reflections, which you may wish to play (again) at the end of the session. Do whatever is best for you and your group.

SESSION 1

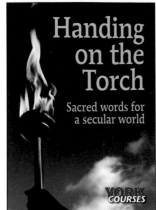

Handing
on the
Torch

Sacred words for
a secular world

YORK
COURSES

A CHRISTIAN COUNTRY?

It is up to Christians to show by the gracious and conscientious fulfilment of their duties that our presence and witness is to be welcomed, not feared. We cannot expect the law to do this for us.

Professor Julian Rivers

Despite protests from churches, several cities plan to introduce expensive Sunday car-parking charges. These threaten congregational life and in some cases (e.g. the Salvation Army) social action. Some church-goers are considering standing for election as local councillors to combat this.

In the presence of suffering, prayer is often the only language left to us. *Anon*

A golden age?

In the spring of 1910 the tides on the river Thames, and the term dates of Oxford and Cambridge Universities, meant that the famous annual boat race was held during Holy Week. There was a rumpus. In the end the race was held, but the usual dinner wasn't, and all official invitations to places of entertainment were declined. By common consent, Holy Week was to be honoured, preserved and protected.

A bygone age indeed! Though if that's what is meant by 'a Christian country', many modern Christians will feel glad to live in less buttoned-up times.

The pendulum swings

The pendulum has swung a very long way in a hundred years. In 'post-Christian Britain' many believers feel that their views and sensibilities count for nothing. Some even feel that their faith is actively targeted or belittled:

- Staff working in various organisations have been suspended for wearing crosses
- A teacher was disciplined for offering prayer
- A Christian counsellor was sacked for refusing to work on sexual issues with a gay couple
- A Roman Catholic agency with a distinguished record of placing 'unwanted' children for adoption was threatened with closure, because it refused to place children with gay couples
- Some NHS Trusts are considering cutting the provision of hospital chaplains
- A mental-health worker says she was 'bullied out of a job' after showing an anti-abortion booklet to a colleague
- At a more rarefied level, there's a lobby to remove bishops from the House of Lords

It is important – and fascinating – to trace possible reasons for this immense change in public attitude over just three or four generations. Here are a few:

'... wars and rumours of wars ...' (Mark 13.7)

The so-called 'Great War' of 1914-18 saw a huge swing in public mood. The optimism with which many had volunteered for the trenches died in the mud and the slaughter – and with the arrival of the telegrams. Authority figures were no longer deferred to without question. Theologians came to a deeper understanding of the seriousness of sin and the reality of evil. Deep questions surfaced in many minds. People were less inclined to accept received wisdom about God and the state of the world.

In the trenches, chaplains received a mixed response. Some commanded deep respect and affection. Most famous was the poet-chaplain Geoffrey Studdert Kennedy ('Woodbine Willie'). But not all chaplains aspired to his heroic standards. As deference declined, acceptance of the Church's authority loosened.

This process continued through and after the Second World War. Despite this, the Christian faith played a key role for many as they survived the war and rebuilt their lives. Many men returned from active service to offer themselves for ordination. Christopher Lees-Smith (who became the Franciscan, Brother Edward) was one of these. His father held high office as Postmaster General, and Christopher himself had been on course for a high-powered political career.

When Brother Edward died on 25 February 2010, an obituary explained why he changed direction: '*The Second World War interrupted his education. He achieved rapid promotion, having served in the Territorial Army before the war, and was among the liberators of Belsen concentration camp in 1945. The horrors of that experience changed his life, and he abandoned politics for ordination in the Church of England.*'

The structures of society were changing. With so many men in the armed forces, women did 'men's work' during the war. In 1945, when it was over, it was widely assumed that they would return to the kitchen sink. They did return (in one sense, they'd never left it!) but horizons had been raised. Today's working mothers and career women bear witness to this – though surveys show that women still undertake the major share of domestic chores and family responsibilities, even when both partners are in paid employment.

Holocaust, earthquakes and the media

At an intellectual level the big questions continue to press in. 'Where was God during the Holocaust?' was one huge question raised by World War II. The questions raised by suffering are still with us. Our world has always been marked by earthquakes and tsunamis. In a world 'built' on tectonic plates, this is inevitable. But for centuries people were aware only of disasters near to home. Now we learn of far-off catastrophes as soon as they happen. So the questions are kept alive – and easygoing faith is challenged. No bad thing, perhaps?

Except that one easygoing faith has been replaced by another. Many of today's young people (and not so young too) believe without question that organized religion has nothing to offer. When I grew up in the Sunday-school generation, the majority of children had personal experience of their local church. Many young people today have never even entered a church building.

The car and the telly

The advent of the cheap production-line car opened up possibilities for family outings. As many worked on Saturday mornings, Sunday became the only free full day. Then came the telly, popularized in 1953 with the Coronation of Queen Elizabeth II – and universalized soon after. Some observers argued that the television serialization of John Galsworthy's *The Forsyte Saga* on Sundays (in 1967) killed evening services in many parish churches, in those far-off days before recording programmes was possible.

The practice of attending church more than once on a Sunday is now fairly rare, even among committed Christians.

Issues of life and death

The decades since 1945 have seen many changes. Increasing affluence in Britain is one (though a large number of children are still officially in poverty). The rise in litigation – imported from the USA – is another. Public attitudes to religious faith and family life have changed dramatically.

In 1967 the first Abortion Bill was introduced by David Steel – a Christian MP. The focus of debate has broadened to include stem-cell research and 'end of life' issues. There is widespread support for assisted suicide (some prefer the phrase 'assisted death') and euthanasia. The long-held Christian view of 'the sanctity of human life' is giving way to: 'It's *my* life and *my* death, let *me* choose'.

There is no single Christian approach to any of these questions. The Roman Catholic Church – together with fundamentalist Christians – officially takes a conservative position on most of these issues. But the traditionalist stance of the Vatican is at variance with many members of its laity, who tend to be more liberal and accepting.

Many modern Christians believe that the Roman Catholic Church is profoundly wrong in opposing the use of condoms in a world where HIV/AIDS is rampant, and promiscuity is widespread. The Pope seemed to open the door to further debate on this, in an interview in November 2010.

Sex 'n' drugs 'n' rock 'n' roll

The 1960s famously gave rise to a new postwar generation with a different mindset. The arrival of 'the pill' removed fear of unwanted pregnancy and led to the sexual revolution. Authority figures – including senior clerics – were questioned and sometimes mocked. The 'deferential society' crumbled. Gay men and women found a voice following the decriminalization of homosexuality in 1967, as recommended in the Wolfenden Report of 1957.

Bill Haley and his Comets had teenagers dancing (literally) in the aisles in cinemas. Along came Elvis (with his gospel background), the Beatles (who famously followed a Hindu guru for a while), and the Rolling Stones (who didn't!). Then came the Sex Pistols. Pop music and drugs were closely associated in many minds, anticipating the drug problem prevalent today.

We now live in a highly sexualized society. In 2009 NHS Sheffield produced a sex booklet for teenagers entitled *Pleasure*. It advises teenagers of their 'right to an enjoyable sex-life'. It suggests that along with '5 portions of fruit and veg a day ... what about sex or masturbation twice a week?'. This was described by the ecumenical Maranatha Community as 'a form of child abuse'. They added, 'the foundations of Western society are collapsing'.

We've certainly travelled a long way in a few years. This journey has brought many problems – and many benefits too. A less open, more hierarchical society is not necessarily a better – or more Christian – society than a freewheeling one. Like it or not, this is our fast-moving world. This is the world we are called to love and serve in the strength of the risen Christ – and to witness to in his name.

A Theos survey for Easter 2008 showed that:
- 57% of Britons believe Jesus rose from the dead
- 66% think 'Jesus was a good man and wise teacher'
- 47% think 'Jesus was a holy prophet'
- 40% think 'Jesus was the son of God'
- 13% think 'Jesus never existed'

QUESTIONS FOR GROUPS

BIBLE READING: Micah 6.6-8

Some groups will address all the questions. That's fine. Others prefer to select just a few and spend longer on each. That's fine, too. Horses for (York) Courses!

1. Reminisce! How does modern childhood compare with your own? Do we over-protect children today – or perhaps expose them to too much risk?

2. 'Women still undertake the major share of domestic chores and family responsibilities.' Is this true in your experience? Are things different – or *should* things be different – in Christian families?

3. Holy Week was highly significant a century ago. How do you personally observe Holy Week (if you do) and how would you like your church to observe it?

4. Two world wars raised questions about a loving God – yet many people came to faith. On the course CD and transcript Archbishop Sentamu tells us how he hung onto a Bible verse when his life was in danger under Idi Amin. How has suffering affected your faith – and how has your faith helped in times of suffering (if it has)?

5. Re-read Brian Sewell's words (box p. 4). Do you agree? Where do you stand on assisted suicide and euthanasia? Do you believe we have a moral right to choose the time and manner of our own death?

6. Do you wear a cross/display a symbol (e.g. fish car sticker) as an act of Christian witness? Is the fuss about 'crosses at work' a fuss about nothing – or an important point of principle?

7. 'Many Christians believe that the Roman Catholic Church is profoundly wrong in opposing the use of condoms in a world where HIV/AIDS is rampant, and promiscuity is widespread.' Some Catholics – including Clifford Longley on the course CD and transcript – hold a more liberal view than the Vatican. What do *you* think?

8. Today's young people are growing up in a highly sexualized society. What do you make of the quote from the NHS Sheffield booklet for teenagers (p. 5) – and the response of the Maranatha Community?

9. Should mothers have the right to know if their teenage daughters are being prescribed contraceptives?

10. A Pentecostal Christian couple with a distinguished record as foster-parents were removed from the approved list because of their traditional beliefs regarding homosexuality. The couple asked, 'Do Christians have to compromise their faith to be foster-parents?' Well, do they?

Archbishop Rowan spoke feelingly about his [2011] visit to Congo, where he had heard victims and perpetrators of violence who had been rescued by the Church there. 'And I thought, listening to them, "If it wasn't for the Church, no one, absolutely no one, would have cared, and they would be lost still." … It put into perspective the fashionable sneers that the Church here lives with, the various excuses people make for not taking seriously the idea that God's incalculable love for every person is the only solid foundation for a human dignity that is beyond question. And it put into a harsh light the self-indulgence of so much of our church life which provides people with just the excuses they need for not taking God seriously. It left me wanting to be a Christian. It left me thinking that there is nothing on earth so transforming as a Church in love.'

SESSION 2

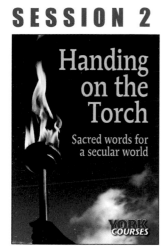

Handing on the Torch

Sacred words for a secular world

YORK COURSES

A SECULAR SOCIETY?

> A real Christian is not only a good and well-intentioned person but a man or woman for whom Jesus Christ is ultimately decisive; for whom Jesus – not Caesar, not another god, not money, sex, power, or pleasure – is Lord.
>
> *Professor Hans Küng*

> I'm a Christian and, at the risk of sounding like a lunatic, I think God has been enormously kind to me ... People who are negative towards Christianity assume you think you're perfect and homophobic. To me, a Christian is someone who has accepted that they don't have all the answers.
>
> *Comic actress, Sally Phillips*

The default position in Britain for much of my life was 'Christian'. Most people put 'C of E' on official forms without much thought. To say that someone wasn't a Christian would usually be viewed as an implied insult.

Today, many public figures are keen to affirm their atheism. Opposition to religion is found in books, on radio and TV and – some would allege – in public policies too. At the same time, many people describe themselves as 'spiritual' rather than 'religious'. The Religious Experience Research Unit, established in 1969 by the scientist Sir Alister Hardy, continues to report that a significant number of people claim to have had a spiritual or religious experience. This is the 'mixed' society in which we live, and in which the Church must stand or fall. The picture is broadly similar in most Western European countries, and other English-speaking nations in which this course will be followed.

A superstitious society

Despite the high-profile efforts of Richard Dawkins, Philip Pullman and other well-known atheists, we have not become a society of hardheaded rationalists. The National Secular Society and the British Humanist Association are active, but their membership remains low. Polls show that large numbers continue to believe in God, in prayer, and in angels. Huge numbers are superstitious, basing decisions on horoscopes.

Yes, we are a secular society in the sense that our public life is not conducted as 'in the sight of God'. But 'secular' does not do justice to the prevailing mindset. Perhaps the phrase 'secular, spiritual and superstitious' sums up our society rather more accurately. Not much comfort here for Christians though. People who describe themselves as spiritual sometimes add 'but not religious', in order to distance themselves from the Church. And superstition can be an even tougher opponent than secularism.

A tolerant society?

Ask people which personal qualities are most important and many will answer 'a sense of humour' and 'tolerance'. But in practice we're not a very tolerant, 'live and let live' society.

Take that Roman Catholic adoption agency mentioned in Session 1. Must we enforce uniformity? For the law to decree that gay couples can make good parents is one thing. For the law to insist that *all* adoption agencies must be willing to place children with gay couples is quite another. In practice, of course, gay couples wanting to adopt are unlikely to approach a Catholic agency! So one argument runs: why not let the Catholic agency do what it's good at – finding good heterosexual homes for young children who are difficult to place? This practical solution would keep the

7

agency in business – to the immense benefit of very needy children. Against this, others claim that this course of action would have unintended consequences – insulting gay parents and placing a 'second-class citizen' approach on the statute books. In response, some would argue that we already have that – with Christians as the second-class citizens.

A multi-racial society

Recently I attended a school reunion. Getting off the tube at Hounslow East I found that little had changed. I saw the same buildings as when I walked those streets 60 years ago. The familiar bus station which I knew so well, and used so often, was as busy as ever.

Yet at the same time, everything was different. In many of the shops I could buy Asian food served by Asian shopkeepers. Halal meat was readily available – a term which I never heard as a teenager. I felt sure that many people walking those streets were firm in faith and devout in practice. British Christians are often challenged by the open, unembarrassed piety of their neighbours who follow a different creed.

Secular Britain can be confused by this. A couple of years ago library staff in Sunderland refused to display a poster advertising the (Christian) Women's World Day of Prayer. They felt it might cause offence to people of other faiths.

In fact, most Muslims, Jews, Sikhs – and members of Britain's many other faith communities – greatly value the vestiges of Christian culture left in Britain. They encourage us to celebrate our festivals. Many appreciate an 'established religion' – including bishops in the House of Lords, believing that in one sense they represent and safeguard *all* people of faith. The Prince of Wales famously wants to change the Monarch's title from 'Defender of the Faith' to 'Defender of Faith'.

A fearful society?

Is our society growing more violent? At first sight it is. Turf wars between rival gangs lead to deaths by shooting and stabbing. Some elderly people stay indoors whenever possible. In fact violent crime is relatively low. And a male teenager is more likely to be the victim of a violent attack than a pensioner is.

As a child I was free to play in the streets and roam the countryside. Necessary concern about traffic accidents has curbed that easygoing parental attitude. But there is another concern fuelling this same caution: the constant worry about the lurking paedophile. Yes, they do exist. They existed in my childhood too. But most abusers are family members or friends – not strangers waiting to pounce.

In Britain new religions have become more accepted. The Prison Service recognises Pagan chaplains; devotees of the International Society for Krishna Consciousness contribute to *Thought for the Day*.

Professor Eileen Barker

My parents kept a low profile, feeling that we were guests here, but my generation – we're not guests ... We thought things could only get better. Some have. [However] Muslims are tired of being mocked and abused ... we don't insult Moses or Jesus, because they're our prophets, too. Leave our faith alone.

Khola Hasan, writer and broadcaster

The Community Security Trust (CST) reported that there were 639 'anti-Semitic incidents' in the UK in 2010 – the second-highest number since records began in 1984.

The rioting in several English cities in August 2011 led many people to reflect on the fragility of community life. 'Clean-up groups', seeking to restore calm and order, quickly sprang up.

Yet even writing this feels dangerous, in another sense. A healthy society is founded on (sensible) trust – not widespread suspicion that views everyone as a possible threat. In fact, the risks are statistically low, and there is no such thing as a risk-free life. Some observers feel that our approach is over-cautious – perhaps even repressive.

In an attempt to safeguard children, in 2009 the government proposed widespread vetting procedures – treating everyone as a possible suspect. Some argue that this is too complex and heavy-handed. Philip Pullman famously objected to having to get 'clearance' to read from his books at occasional 'Meet the Author' sessions in schools.

Whatever the merits of these vetting procedures, other dangers lurk within our homes. In the privacy of their own bedrooms children log on to social networking sites such as Facebook, and join internet chat rooms where they can 'meet' strangers. All this can be enriching but – like all good things – it can be abused. 'Cyber-bullying' is a related problem, as is the naïve disclosure of personal details.

An unstable society?

Some commentators date the decline of the Christian Church from the 1960s, with the sexual revolution and the demise of the deferential society. One outcome has been the weakening of marriage as the bedrock of society. Divorce is common and a range of alternatives to marriage has grown up, some of them recognized in law. Many – including some Christians – argue that these developments have brought benefits. Yet it's clear that some children have suffered from this flexibility.

An ageing society

Many countries – especially in the Middle East and the developing world – have huge numbers of children and young people. In contrast, Britain now has more over-60s than under-16s.

In many ways this is positive. It means that we are living longer, healthier lives. But increasing numbers of elderly people will need a lot of care. Who will do the caring? And who will pay for the care? These are crucial questions which will occupy many governmental minds for decades to come.

Just a few years ago, the last surviving combatants from the First World War were laid to rest. They were honoured and admired; their funerals were televised. Whether they were personally devout or not, they were at home in a Christian culture. They knew the hymns; they were comfortable in church. They expected – and wanted – the Church to be involved in acts of Remembrance. Have those days gone for ever?

'The times they are a-changin',' sang Bob Dylan. He was right, all right!

QUESTIONS FOR GROUPS
BIBLE READING: 1 Peter 2.13-25

1. Pope Benedict urged parents to choose 'proper' Christian names for their children. What do you think about this?

2. Not so long ago a man married a woman – or they remained single. No longer! Do you welcome or lament today's options (civil partnerships; cohabitation; same sex parents; surrogate mothers ...)? Is this wider range good for, or harmful to, our children?

3. On the course CD and transcript Rachel Lampard and Clifford Longley consider whether gay rights should always take priority over Christian conscience. What do you think? A Roman Catholic adoption agency now threatened with closure under human rights legislation has served children for 140 years. Rather than close, should it sacrifice its principles (about not accepting gay couples as parents) for the sake of children awaiting adoption?

4. In our ageing society is pastoral church care for the elderly good, bad or indifferent in your experience? How might we improve it? As you consider your own old age, is your faith in God a help and comfort?

5. 'A significant number of people claim to have had a spiritual or religious experience.' Have you – or has anyone known to you? If you're willing, please share with your group. How did/does this affect your/their life?

6. 'For much of my long life to say someone wasn't a Christian would usually be viewed as an insult.' You're invited to write down your definition of 'a Christian' and share with your group. You might find it helpful to illustrate from your own journey to faith.

7. You're challenged by a sceptical friend: 'Do you *really* believe in God, in prayer, and in angels? If so, why?' Share your views and any uncertainties.

8. A friend says she is 'spiritual but not religious' and asks what you get out of organized religion (i.e. church). What would you say?

9. 'British Christians are often challenged by the open, unembarrassed piety of their neighbours who follow a different creed.' Should we Christians be a bit more open about our own belief in Jesus Christ? How might we do this boldly, yet sensitively?

10. 'Most members of Britain's many other faith communities greatly value the vestiges of Christian culture left in Britain'. Is this true in your experience? Is conversation between Britain's various faith communities to be welcomed? If so, how might we foster this?

11. Church schools have a fine academic track record. They also claim to help under-privileged children and to further good community relations. Should we encourage faith schools (of all religions) or is this likely to be divisive?

12. In his Closing Reflection on the course CD Bishop Graham Cray suggests that the challenge for Christians is not secularism but ignorance – with a third of adults in England never having been to church. He adds, 'We need to sow the story of Jesus back into our nation's memory and imagination.' How might we do this?

SESSION 3

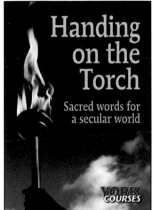

Handing
on the
Torch

Sacred words for
a secular world

WORK COURSES

A BELEAGUERED CHURCH? ✓

> Christianity is the largest, most influential movement of all time. Christians (some more convinced and committed than others, of course) make up about 33% of the world's population. Muslims make up about 21%, Hindus 13%, Buddhists 6%, Jews 0.2%.
>
> *Christianity –*
> *An Introduction (Hodder)*

> The Governor of Karnataka in India noted (in 2010) that despite making up 2.3 per cent of India's 1.2 billion population, Christians ran nearly 20 per cent of the country's education, health and welfare centres. 'Christians have truly followed the message of love preached by Christ by serving people with the spirit of sacrifice.'

A declining Church

Some years ago I travelled the length of Turkey, visiting the Seven Churches of Asia Minor celebrated in Revelation, the last book of the Bible. When John wrote this famous Apocalypse, these were well-known, vigorous churches.

Perhaps their apparent strength carried the seeds of their downfall, for those strong churches did not last. Modern Turkey is officially a secular state, though many of its citizens are deeply religious. As in every country on the globe, you can find Christian believers. But in Turkey ('Asia Minor') they are a small minority among the Muslim majority.

Western Christians might helpfully reflect on these once influential churches. Jesus assures us that the gates of death and hell cannot overcome the Church (Matthew 16.18). But he gives no guarantee to any *particular* church, whether local or national. As Jesus said more than once, 'Those who have ears to hear, let them hear!'

Since my ordination 40 years ago the Church in Britain has steadily declined. (So much for the fruitfulness of my ministry!) Many reasons have been put forward to explain this decline – and we looked at some of the longer-term reasons in Session 1. Church leaders and sociologists also point to:

- *Individualism*: We are no longer a society of 'joiners'; we prefer to 'do our own thing'. Political parties, trades unions – and churches – are all on the sharp end of this.
- *Secularisation*: One outcome is the 'busy Sunday'. For decades, the churches were in a privileged position. Today, there are many alternatives on offer – from Sunday shopping to countless Sunday football leagues for children and teenagers.
- *'Affluenza'*: With rising living standards and increasing wealth over the decades, we've become more materialistic. The current global financial crisis has rocked our confidence, but not fundamentally changed our outlook. Growing affluence was not shared by everyone. Many families in modern Britain still live below the official poverty line – with 'fuel poverty' experienced by a growing number.

Recent figures suggest that the decline in UK church attendance might be slowing. Certainly many churches are growing. But all the statistics – and the evidence of our eyes – suggest that attendance by *young* people is declining. What might this mean for the future?

A committed Church

Decline does have some advantages. Those who attend are there because that's where they want to be. Attending church on Sunday is no longer 'the thing to do'. Indeed, it is often viewed as a rather wacky minority interest.

A humble Church

History suggests that power and influence are not always good for the health of the Church's soul. Because we no longer enjoy such a privileged position in society, perhaps we're able to keep closer to Jesus who had 'nowhere to lay his head' (Luke 9.58).

But there's another, sadder, reason for our humility. We have been humbled. Humbled in the most dramatic and terrible way. Jesus had a special place in his teaching – and in his heart – for children. He uttered strong words of judgement on those who abused, or were indifferent to, the welfare of 'little ones' (Mark 9.42). Yet the child abuse scandals show that his teaching has been flouted by some leaders within the Church itself.

Priests in the Roman Catholic Church have been the main (though not the only) offenders. But in these ecumenical days, in the public imagination all Churches are tarred with the same brush. A Catholic commentator suggested that the recent scandals about abuse and cover-up have precipitated a crisis of Reformation proportions within the Catholic Church.

Deep concern has been shown towards those who suffered and in 2010 the Pope made a formal apology. But many who have been abused feel that this was too little, far too late. Public respect and affection for the Church has, understandably, been undermined by these appalling crimes.

A divided Church

In its heyday the ecumenical movement was optimistic about church unity. Today this appears to be on the back burner. The successful visit of Pope Benedict to the UK

YORK COURSES
ECUMENICAL COURSES FOR ENQUIRING MINDS

...bringing leading Christian thinkers into your discussion groups

HANDING ON THE TORCH
Sacred words for a secular world

Course booklet written by Canon John Young

FIVE SESSIONS: A Christian Country? A Secular Society?
A Beleaguered Church? Competing Creeds?
Handing on the Torch

Christianity is the largest movement our world has ever
seen. It continues to grow at an immense pace – especially
in Asia (including China), Africa and Latin America. At the
same time, Christianity in the West struggles to grow and –
perhaps – even to survive. In this course we consider some of the reasons
for this and what it might mean for individual Christians, for churches and for
Western culture, in a world where alternative beliefs are increasingly on offer.

*With **Archbishop Sentamu, Clifford Longley, Rachel Lampard.**
Introduced by **Dr David Hope**. Closing Reflections by **Bishop Graham Cray.***

PRICES FOR OUR COURSES

ALL PRICES HELD UNTIL 1st JUNE 2012
FREE 2nd CLASS P&P IN THE UK

BOOKLET: £3.75   *(£3.25 each for 5 or more)*
CD: £10.99   *(£8.99 each for 2 or more)*
AUDIOTAPE: £8.99 *(£6.99 each for 5 or more)*
TRANSCRIPT: £4.99 *(£2.99 each for 2 or more)*

CD TASTER PACK: £17.50 *(1 booklet, 1 CD,
1 transcript)* **worth £19.73 – save £2.23**
BUY ONLINE AND SAVE!

Each group needs 1 CD or audiotape, plus a course
booklet for each member. In addition many groups
find the transcript booklet extremely helpful. The
COURSE BOOKLET has five chapters, each with
questions aimed at provoking wide-ranging
discussion. The **COURSE CD** (or audiotape)
consists of five sessions of approximately 14
minutes each, in the style of a radio programme,
during which each participant contributes. The
words as spoken on the CD/audiotape for the
course are set out in the **TRANSCRIPT** – ideal for
group leaders when preparing. It also cross-
references with the track numbers on the CD
– making it simple to find the start of each new
question put to the participants.

RICH INHERITANCE
Jesus' legacy of love

Course booklet written by Bishop Stephen Cottrell
FIVE SESSIONS: An Empty Tomb; A Group of People;
A Story; A Power; A Meal

Jesus left no written instructions. He didn't seem to have a
plan. At the end, as he hung dying on the cross, almost all of his followers had abandoned him. By
most worldly estimates his ministry was a failure. Nevertheless, Jesus' message of reconciliation with
God lives on. With this good news his disciples changed the world. How did they do it? What else
did Jesus leave behind – what is his 'legacy of love'?

*with **Archbishop Vincent Nichols, Paula Gooder, Jim Wallis**. Introduced by **Dr David Hope**.
Closing Reflections by **Inderjit Bhogal**.*

OUR EASY-TO-USE COURSES FOR GROUP DISCUS

WHEN I SURVEY...
Christ's cross and ours

FIVE SESSIONS: Darkness at Noon; Into Great Silence; The Child on the Cross; Outside a City Wall; Touching the Rock

The death of Christ is a dominant and dramatic theme in the New Testament. The death of Jesus is not the end of a track – it's the gateway into life.

*with **General Sir Richard Dannatt, John Bell, Christina Baxter**. Introduced by **Dr David Hope**. Closing Reflections by **Colin Morris**. Course booklet written by the **Revd Dr John Pridmore**.*

These three... FAITH, HOPE & LOVE

FIVE SESSIONS: Believing and trusting; The Peace of God; Faith into Love; The Greatest of these; All shall be well

Based on the three great qualities celebrated in 1 Corinthians 13.

*with **Bishop Tom Wright, Anne Atkins, The Abbot of Worth**. Closing Reflections by **Professor Frances Young**. Introduced by **Dr David Hope***

THE LORD'S PRAYER
praying it, meaning it, living it

FIVE SESSIONS: Our Father; Thy will be done; Our daily bread; As we forgive; In heaven

In the Lord's Prayer Jesus gives us a pattern for living as his disciples. It also raises vital questions for today's world in which 'daily bread' is uncertain for billions and a refusal to 'forgive those who trespass against us' escalates violence.

*with **Canon Margaret Sentamu, Bishop Kenneth Stevenson, Dr David Wilkinson**. Closing Reflections by **Dr Elaine Storkey**. Introduced by **Dr David Hope***

CAN WE BUILD A BETTER WORLD?

FIVE SESSIONS: Slavery – then and now; Friendship & Prayer – then and now; Change & Struggle – then and now; The Bible – then and now; Redemption & Restitution – then and now

We live in a divided world and with a burning question. As modern Christians can we – together with others of good will – build a better world? Important material for important issues.

*with **Archbishop John Sentamu, Wendy Craig, Leslie Griffiths**. Five Poor Clares from BBC TV's The Convent. Introduced by **Dr David Hope***

WHERE IS GOD...?

FIVE SESSIONS: Where is God when we ... seek happiness? ... face suffering? ... make decisions? ... contemplate death? ... try to make sense of life?

To find honest answers to these big questions we need to undertake some serious and open thinking. Where better to do this than with trusted friends in a study group around this course?

*with **Archbishop Rowan Williams, Patricia Routledge** CBE, **Joel Edwards, Dr Pauline Webb**. Introduced by **Dr David Hope***

BETTER TOGETHER?

FIVE SESSIONS: Family Relationships; Church Relationships; Relating to Strangers; Broken Relationships; Our Relationship with God

All about relationships – in the church and within family and society. *Better Together?* looks at how the Christian perspective may differ from that of society at large.

*with **the Abbot of Ampleforth, John Bell, Nicky Gumbel, Jane Williams**. Introduced by **Dr David Hope***

TOUGH TALK Hard Sayings of Jesus

FIVE SESSIONS: Shrinking and Growing; Giving and Using; Praying and Forgiving; Loving and Telling; Trusting and Entering

Looks at many of the hard sayings of Jesus in the Bible and faces them squarely. His uncomfortable words need to be faced if we are to allow the full impact of the gospel on our lives.

ARE SUITABLE FOR LENT – OR ANY TIME OF YEAR

with *Bishop Tom Wright, Steve Chalke, Fr Gerard Hughes SJ, Professor Frances Young.* Introduced by *Dr David Hope*

NEW WORLD, OLD FAITH

FIVE SESSIONS: Brave New World?; Environment and Ethics; Church and Family in Crisis?; One World – Many Faiths; Spirituality and Superstition

How does Christian faith continue to shed light on a range of issues in our changing world, including change itself? This course helps us make sense of our faith in God in today's world.

with *Archbishop Rowan Williams, David Coffey, Joel Edwards, Revd Dr John Polkinghorne* KBE FRS, *Dr Pauline Webb.* Introduced by *Dr David Hope*

IN THE WILDERNESS

FIVE SESSIONS: Jesus, Satan and the Angels; The Wilderness Today; The Church in the Wilderness; Prayer, Meditation and Scripture; Solitude, Friendship and Fellowship

Like Jesus, we all have wilderness experiences. What are we to make of these challenges? *In the Wilderness* explores these issues for our world, for the church, and at a personal level.

with *Cardinal Cormac Murphy-O'Connor, Archbishop David Hope, Revd Dr Rob Frost, Roy Jenkins, Dr Elaine Storkey*

FAITH IN THE FIRE

FIVE SESSIONS: Faith facing Facts; Faith facing Doubt; Faith facing Disaster; Faith fuelling Prayer; Faith fuelling Action

When things are going well our faith may remain untroubled, but what if doubt or disaster strike? Those who struggle with faith will find they are not alone.

with *Archbishop David Hope, Rabbi Lionel Blue, Steve Chalke, Revd Dr Leslie Griffiths, Ann Widdecombe* MP

JESUS REDISCOVERED

FIVE SESSIONS: Jesus' Life and Teaching; Following Jesus; Jesus: Saviour of the World; Jesus is Lord; Jesus and the Church

Re-discovering who Jesus was, what he taught, and what that means for his followers today. Some believers share what Jesus means to them.

with *Paul Boateng* MP, *Dr Lavinia Byrne, Joel Edwards, Bishop Tom Wright, Archbishop David Hope*

LIVE YOUR FAITH

SIX SESSIONS: The Key - Jesus; Prayer; The Community - the Church; The Dynamic - the Holy Spirit; The Bible; The Outcome - Service & Witness

Christianity isn't just about what we believe: it's about how we live. A course suitable for everyone; particularly good for enquirers and those in the early stages of their faith.

with *Revd Dr Donald English, Lord Tonypandy, Fiona & Roy Castle*

GREAT EVENTS, DEEP MEANINGS

SIX SESSIONS: Christmas; Ash Wednesday; Palm Sunday; Good Friday; Easter; Pentecost

Explains clearly what the feasts and fasts are about and challenges us to respond spiritually and practically. There are even a couple of quizzes to get stuck into!

with *Revd Dr John Polkinghorne* KBE FRS, *Gordon Wilson, Bishop David Konstant, Fiona Castle, Dame Cicely Saunders, Archbishop David Hope*

PRICES FOR OUR COURSES

FREE 2nd CLASS P&P IN THE UK

BOOKLET: £3.75   (*£3.25 each for 5 or more*)
CD: £10.99   (*£8.99 each for 2 or more*)
AUDIOTAPE: £8.99 (*£6.99 each for 5 or more*)
TRANSCRIPT: £4.99 (*£2.99 each for 2 or more*)

CD TASTER PACK: £17.50 – save £2.23

2 PHOTOCOPYABLE COURSES

ATTENDING, EXPLORING, ENGAGING

with **Archbishop David Hope, Steve Chalke, Fr Gerard Hughes SJ, Professor Frances Young**

FIVE SESSIONS: Attending to God; Attending to One Another; Exploring Our Faith; Engaging with the World in Service; Engaging with the World in Evangelism

THE TEACHING OF JESUS

with **Steve Chalke, Professor James Dunn, Dr Pauline Webb, Archbishop David Hope**

FIVE SESSIONS: Forgiveness; God; Money; Heaven and Hell; On Being Human

Comprising photocopyable notes, audiotape and photocopyable transcript

AUDIOTAPE: £8.99 (£6.99 each for 5 or more)
TRANSCRIPT: £4.99
PHOTOCOPYABLE NOTES: £3.25

CD CONVERSATIONS

ROWAN REVEALED

The Archbishop of Canterbury talks about his life and faith, prayer, the press, politics, the future of the Church ...

CD	**£3.50**
Transcript	**£2.99**

SCIENCE AND CHRISTIAN FAITH £5

An in-depth discussion with the Revd Dr John Polkinghorne KBE FRS, former Professor of Mathematical Physics at Cambridge University.

CLIMATE CHANGE AND CHRISTIAN FAITH £5

Nobel Prize winner Sir John Houghton CBE, FRS, a world expert on global warming, talks about why he believes in Climate Change and in Jesus Christ.

PRAYER £3.50

Archbishop David Hope on *Prayer*. Four Christians on praying ... for healing; in danger; in tongues; with perseverance.

This CD accompanies the booklet *The Archbishop's School of Prayer*.

TOPIC TAPES
STRUGGLING/COPING

4 personal conversations – **£5 each tape**
(Both tapes for **£8.50**)

TAPE 1: *Living with ... depression; ... panic attacks*
TAPE 2: *Living with ... cancer; ... bereavement*

FINDING FAITH £1.99

is a 20-minute audiotape, designed for enquirers and church members. Four brief stories by people, including Archbishop David Hope, who have found faith.

Inexpensive! Designed as a 'give away'

Multipacks of CDs available at www.yorkcourses.co.uk

BOOKLETS and BOOKS

ARCHBISHOP'S SCHOOL SERIES

7 BOOKLETS COMMISSIONED BY Dr DAVID HOPE – Prayer; Bible Reading; Evangelism; The Sacraments; Christianity and Science; Healing and Wholeness; Life After Death.

Authors include John Polkinghorne and David Winter **99p** each

Special offer:
Complete set of all 7 booklets only £5

CHRISTIANITY – AN INTRODUCTION £7.99

Special prices for Hodder paperbacks by John Young, author of most of our course booklets.

CHRISTIANITY MADE SIMPLE

NEW

a to-the-point guide in 96 pages.
£4.99

YORK COURSES

York Courses · PO Box 343 York YO19 5YB UK · Tel: 01904 466516
Email: courses@yorkcourses.co.uk
FREE PACKING & 2ND CLASS POSTAGE IN UK
Payment with order please.
Cheques: York Courses

www.yorkcourses.co.uk
for fuller details of all courses:
• download sample booklet pages
• listen to soundbites from our CDs
• latest special offers and discounted prices
• Secure online ordering

VISA · DELTA · Maestro · EUROCARD/MasterCard

in 2010 gave fresh heart to many. But there are some apparently insoluble issues which continue to divide the Churches. These often focus on gender and sex.

A self-absorbed Church?

A letter from senior clerics in *The Daily Telegraph* complained that the Church is being marginalised. Dr Giles Fraser, Canon Chancellor of St Paul's Cathedral, responded: *'There is nothing wrong with using the public stage to try to spread the message of the Kingdom. But to use it endlessly to moan about the fact that people are not listening to or respecting us makes the Church look like a bunch of grumpy old men, upset that they are no longer at the centre of the governing class. No, our message ought to be the power of the risen Christ. If we live in that power, why should we worry? How can we ever lose?'*

He makes an important point. It might be appropriate to remind secular Britain that it has been formed and shaped by Christian values and beliefs, but we have no divine right to a privileged position.

A privileged Church

In fact, privileged is what we still are. Chaplains continue to play an important and widely accepted role in our institutions – from prisons to hospitals; from universities to the Armed Forces. Twenty-six Anglican bishops currently sit in the House of Lords. UK church schools educate around a million children, and most do so with great distinction. We have much to be thankful for – and to build on. Individual Christians, Christian organisations and churches continue to play a significant role in the public arena, especially with the advent of 'The Big Society'.

Perhaps we need to examine our motives. Christian outreach and evangelism cannot properly be motivated solely by a desire to 'keep the show on the road' – as though we are a club threatened with closure. Of course, if we love the Church we want it to thrive into the future. But here, as always, the teaching of Jesus puts us right. If we put survival first, we will die. If we seek to live and share our glorious good news, who knows, we might not merely survive – we might flourish!

A healthy Church?

In 2009 Professor Diarmaid MacCulloch presented a memorable six-part BBC TV series, *The History of*

Street Pastors in Southampton have been praised for helping to significantly decrease the number of violent and alcohol-related crimes at weekends in the city centre. Southampton's police have noticed a 30 per cent reduction in the number of reported crimes relating to night-life in the 18 months since Street Pastors started their work.

In 1925, the poet and theologian Charles Williams [a friend of C S Lewis] was asked what he thought it meant to live the Christian life. Williams replied: 'Love, laugh, pray and be intelligent.'

Revd Peter McGeary

One commentator asked: 'Is it cynical to note that calls for The Big Society come at the same time as cuts to our public services? In other words we are supposed to be taking on things that the Government no longer feels it can pay for, partly because of the massive expenditure on overseas military commitments in Afghanistan, Iraq and Libya.' What do you think?

Christianity. This accompanied an immense book which received rave reviews. He knows what he's talking about. Reflecting on the fast-growing world Church, and the Church of England in which he grew up as a vicar's son, he warns against accepting too readily the media reports which speak of empty churches and a dying faith. We've already noted that many local churches are growing. Overall, there are still more people in UK churches each week than on football terraces. We are far from finished. Perhaps Archbishop Michael Ramsey was right when he spoke of 'the great Christian centuries yet to come'.

A Church with a future?

- 'Christianity is at last discovered to be fictitious... a principal subject of mirth and ridicule'
- 'The Church of England as it now stands no human power can save.'

We need to be realistic. We need to face facts. But perhaps a little history will encourage us. When do you think the words in the first bullet point were written? They fit our age perfectly, but they were in fact penned by Bishop Joseph Butler in 1736. He wrote this with irony in his *Analogy of Religion*, for it described the mood of his time. Yet this was just before the great evangelical revival which ushered in Factory Acts, legislation about child labour, the abolition of the slave trade, and a revival of faith under the Wesley brothers, among others.

And what about the second quotation? The answer is that those words were written in 1832 by the poet Matthew Arnold. He said this just before the Oxford Movement was to revolutionise and galvanise the Church of England to arguably its greatest period. So far, that is! Perhaps the 'God of Surprises' has a few more in store ...

14

QUESTIONS FOR GROUPS

BIBLE READING: Revelation 3.14-22

[handwritten: intolerance   The Barn   Church   Culloden]

1. Your local hospital is about to axe its chaplaincy and two petitions are being circulated (see box below). Would you sign either petition – and why?

> (a) *Keep our chaplain!* There is evidence of a strong link between spiritual welfare and physical health. (b) *Cut the chaplaincy!* Buy an MRI scanner instead. *[handwritten: Secular]*

2. *Reminisce!* How does today's church compare with the church of your childhood? When and how did you become an active member? Share with your group.

3. A short questionnaire to put our situation in a global perspective. (Answers in box at foot of page.)
   a. The Church throughout the world is declining – YES/NO
   b. The fastest growing Church in the world is Anglican/Baptist/ Catholic/Methodist/Orthodox/ Pentecostal

   Now *prophesy*! What do you think the church in your country will be like in 2050 (its size, ministry, influence ...)?

4. Do you know of a local church(es) where attendance is growing? How do they achieve this? Is church growth always good? Are declining churches, failing churches?

5. How can we, as individual churches and as churches working together, encourage young people in our society to develop Christian faith?

6. 'Attending church on Sunday is no longer "the thing to do". Indeed, it is often viewed as a rather wacky minority interest.' Is this true in your experience? Draw up a list of possible reasons why people attend church. Do our motives matter as long as we're there?

7. 'Our message ought to be the power of the risen Christ. If we live in that power, why should we worry? How can we ever lose?' (p. 13). Do you feel the force of Giles Fraser's words in your life and in your church?

8. On the CD, Clifford Longley states his opposition to bishops in the House of Lords. In a box (p. 13) the Methodist Lord Griffiths gives his support to their presence and voice. Where do you stand?

9. Do you want/have strong relations with other churches in your area? How might you improve them? On the CD, Clifford Longley feared the Pope's visit in 2010 might be a 'horror' but praised an 'impressive and moving event'. What was your response to his visit?

10. Issues of gender and sex continue to cause division within the Church. Share your views on women priests and bishops, and on gay laity and clergy. In the face of deep differences of opinion, will the Church ever be united?

11. What are the advantages of celibate clergy? What are the advantages of married clergy?

12. Have you ever considered ordination – or encouraged someone else to consider it? Or should we simply leave it to God to do the calling, without our help?

> Answers to Q. 3 above:
> (a) No, it's growing – fast
> (b) Pentecostalism

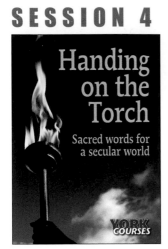

Handing
on the
Torch

Sacred words for
a secular world

YORK
COURSES

COMPETING CREEDS?

> For the last 1,000 years, most people in Christian nations just had one religious choice ...Today people can explore hundreds of expressions of religion and spirituality ... we are, whether we like it or not, in a religious market place.
>
> *Revd Steve Hollinghurst*

> Hertfordshire Police is believed to be the first constabulary to appoint humanist lay advisers to its chaplaincy team. Two members of the British Humanist Association will join the 20-strong team, which includes Christian, Jewish, Muslim and Pagan staff.

Most people don't sign up to a particular creed. They are 'guided' through life by a mixture of intuition, beliefs, convictions, principles and self-interest – and perhaps by a sense that personal fulfilment and happiness is something we all have a right to. But there are a few dominant creeds in Britain today, and in other Western countries too. We'll look at five of these.

Each creed has its own narrative or story. Each of these narratives carries meaning and understanding for its adherents, helping them make sense of life and – in some cases – of death too. In a sense, these creeds are competing for the allegiance of the soul of our nation. There's a huge amount at stake – nothing less than the future shape of our civilisation.

The Atheist Story

Like every belief system, atheism is inescapably based on faith. According to this creed the human race – including you and me – is here on earth by random chance. The physical is everything. The spiritual realm is an illusion. Religion is a fairy story which can be harmful (although some atheists would concede that it does some good). There is no grand design; certainly no Grand Designer. Our existence is a fluke: a happy accident. For a few years – a few decades if we're lucky – we bumble around as best we can. Some people mark up remarkable achievements. Most of us do little of distinction. Then we fall off the edge into oblivion and extinction. Empty Nothingness has the final word.

During our brief lives, we may experience love. Indeed, we may feel 'the call' to love and serve – though there's no one 'out there' to do the calling. All too quickly our ration of years runs out. Death is the end of us. And so each generation is replaced by a new cohort.

As for the human race ... in the end we'll destroy ourselves or, given time, the forces of nature will do that work for us in the big crunch or the slow freeze.

Atheism is a bleak, perhaps brave, creed. But it is not without its attractions. It excludes Divine forgiveness, but it also excludes ultimate accountability. Our sins, and all those shabby actions and attitudes of which we are ashamed, die with us – whatever their ongoing effects in the world of the living may be. Atheism asserts that oblivion greets Hitler as well as Anne Frank; Stalin as well as Mother Teresa.

The Hedonist Story

This is quickly summed up in words based on Luke 12.19 and 1 Corinthians 15.32: *Eat, drink and be merry for tomorrow we die ...* Let's have a party! Or if you prefer a dictionary definition: a hedonist is 'one who believes that pleasure is the chief good in life'. It is closely related to 'materialism', because money can fuel pleasure (we shop – or drink – till we drop).

The New Age Story

There is no single narrative, but its various manifestations have some common features.

The world is an arena for the interaction between the physical and the spiritual. We are wise to take spiritual forces into account, for by tuning into them we can achieve peace of mind and a greater mastery over our lives. For this reason pop star Madonna has 'blessed water' in her central heating – presenting problems to plumbers called in to undertake repairs!

There is no one belief system which is right – each person can chart their own route. And there's no one organization (no 'Church') which can helpfully unite those who subscribe broadly to this approach to life. From the many possibilities on offer, we are free to select the bits which suit us. For this reason it is sometimes called a 'pick 'n' mix' approach.

For some, guidance and truth come through feelings. For others they came through written texts (such as horoscopes) or other devices (like tarot cards or crystals). Or through human agents, such as fortune-tellers. New Agers exhort us to look inward for wisdom, and to do what 'feels good'.

The Christian Story

We are not here by courtesy of blind chance; we've been loved into existence by the God of love. This is true of the entire human race; it is true of you and me. Despite the teeming billions which inhabit our planet, each and every individual is infinitely precious in God's sight. This is the teaching of Jesus, who is God's unique Son.

'Our Heavenly Father', the God to whom Jesus pointed, makes tough demands. Our calling is to live by his agenda of faith, hope and love – not by our own feelings and desires. We are disciples, not free agents. We fail. Often. But by God's grace we are offered forgiveness, a new start and the strength of the Holy Spirit. Jesus ends his great Sermon on the Mount by reminding us that his words are the rock on which the wise build their lives.

The Christian faith does not offer a neat philosophical solution to the problem of suffering. But it does offer strength and comfort. Very often it is people caught up in disasters who show the most robust faith, and who find comfort and sustenance in prayer and worship. The Bible speaks of a suffering God. The New Testament affirms that Jesus died on the cross *for* us; it also assures us that he suffers *with* us. He is alongside us in our pain, for he has been there before us.

When we die, we embark upon the greatest adventure of all: the life of heaven.

The Christian story has much in common with the narratives by which other faith communities live, especially the other two Abrahamic faiths: Judaism and Islam. Some Jews gladly acknowledge Jesus as a fellow Jew. Muslims, drawing on the Qur'an, honour Jesus as a prophet. But they do not worship him as the Son of God, nor accept that God allowed him to die on the cross.

The Muslim Story *

"Islam (meaning submission to the will of the One True God) is one of the three great faiths that sprang from the harsh land and deep silences of the Middle Eastern deserts. The other two are Judaism and Christianity. Unlike Judaism, but like Christianity, Islam is a missionary faith – seeking to win converts.

The creed of Islam is a simple statement in two parts, 'There is no God but Allah, and Muhammad is the messenger of God'.

Being a Muslim is essentially a very personal experience. It cannot be done 'second-hand'. It involves a moment (known as *ihsan* or realization) of being 'born anew'. Every Muslim has to experience this if their Islam is to be a truly living thing.

Most people, once they become aware that God exists, rapidly develop *taqwa* or 'God-consciousness'. They become aware that everything they do, think or say, is done under the 'eyes of God'. It alters everything, from the simplest of deeds to the most momentous.

Muslims believe that they should follow a certain way of life, and do their utmost to carry out a certain set of practices or rituals laid down by God. They believe in, and love, God, and therefore cannot accept a way of life that is too casual – but neither should they try to be extreme in their views and practices. God revealed Islam as not only 'the best of ways' but also as 'the Middle Way'.

Muslims are required to strive to live the most noble and compassionate lives possible. They are urged to be honest, brave, generous, kind-hearted, unselfish, diligent, trustworthy and tolerant.

Muslims, since the lifetime of the Prophet Muhammad, have also been requested by God to perform five religious duties, often known as the 'five pillars of Islam'. These are to bear witness to their belief (by their faith, words and good living), to perform a special prayer five times per day, to fast throughout the daylight hours of the month of Ramadan, to give up a fortieth of their saved wealth every year (once they have taken out that which is needed for their basic requirements and responsibilities), and to make a pilgrimage journey to Makkah [Mecca] at least once in their lifetime."

* Taken from *Islam-An Introduction* by Ruqaiyyah Waris Maqsood (in the *Teach Yourself* series). By kind permission of Hodder Education.

QUESTIONS FOR GROUPS
BIBLE READING: Colossians 3.12-17

1. Discuss the personal spiritual experiences outlined by Clifford Longley (a former atheist), Rachel Lampard and Archbishop Sentamu on tracks 44-46 of the CD, in the light of your own lives and experiences.

2. Pope John Paul spoke out against horoscopes. Why do you think that horoscopes, tarot cards, crystals, fortune-tellers etc are so popular? Are you superstitious? Can a belief in luck or fate be squared with belief in the God of love revealed in Jesus Christ?

3. A young relative is thinking about going to a fortune-teller for guidance or to a spiritualist medium to try to make contact with a dead friend. They ask for your opinion. What would you say?

4. A young person is being 'evangelised' by atheists. She comes to you and asks, 'Why are you a Christian and not an atheist?' How would you respond?

5. Atheism may be a bleak creed, but it has some advantages. Our sins die with us; there is no accountability; no Day of Judgement. Can you feel the attraction of this? How does it compare with the Christian concept of forgiveness of sins?

6. Re-read 'The Muslim Story'. Group members are invited to pick out and share one or two points they find particularly striking or significant.

7. A librarian wearing a burqa tried to help a man with hearing difficulties. Not being able to see her lips, he had great difficulty in communicating with her. Should we forbid such clothing – as in France? Or is wearing clothes of our own choice an important freedom?

8. Should the Muslim call of the faithful to prayer sound out over our villages, towns and cities, alongside church bells?

9. 'By accident we've just tumbled into existence' (Prof. Peter Atkins). In your view, does it take a greater leap of faith to believe our universe – and human life itself – is here by a lucky fluke, or by the will of God? Why?

10. Which is the toughest opponent for Christianity in your country, in your view: apathy, atheism, hedonism, ignorance, materialism, superstition ... ?

11. A Japanese visitor with little knowledge of Christianity asks you to outline the Christian story. As a group consider the main elements that should be included.

12. Christians sometimes complain that people ridicule their faith while being more polite about other faiths. Do you feel the force of this? Does it matter anyway – or is God big enough to look after himself?

13. Baroness Warsi, co-chair of the Tory Party, claims that prejudice against Muslims has 'passed the dinner-table test' and become socially acceptable in the UK. Do you have experience of 'Islamophobia' – in other people, or perhaps in yourself? How can we as Christians help to combat this?

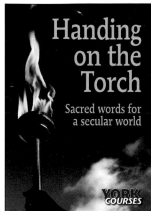

HANDING ON THE TORCH

> There can be no widespread evangelisation of England unless the work is undertaken by the lay people of the Church.
>
> *Archbishop William Temple (1881-1944)*
>
> *
>
> Most of us are fairly comfortable to be disciples – sitting at the Master's feet and learning from him, even though the teaching itself can be tough. We are often less comfortable to be apostles or witnesses – sharing our faith with others.
>
> *John Young*

> In the Bible the call is not primarily to proclaim the gospel, but to live it – 'be holy as I am holy'. Responsibility in mission can be exercised only as a service to the world, in humility and love.
>
> *Bishop Peter Forster*

This then is our task. Just as it has been the task of Jesus' disciples in every generation, since Mary Magdalene encountered the risen Lord in the Garden on that first Easter morning. Jesus gave her an instruction: 'Go and tell' (John 20.17). Like Mary, we have been entrusted with the flame of faith. Our task is to keep it burning and to pass it on. But how? Here are a few pointers.

Learning from the Bible

The early Christians received the good news of God's Kingdom and passed it on very effectively. How did they do this? They got on with their lives (many of them were slaves), they loved their neighbours, welcomed newcomers and talked about their faith when opportunity arose (1 Peter 3.15). This is how they started the rumour of a loving God revealed in Jesus Christ. It wasn't rocket science. Nor is keeping the rumour alive!

They were committed to each other, as well as to Jesus Christ. They shared possessions, prayed together and enjoyed friendship. They were good organisers. Within a few decades they were administering a huge – and much needed – food aid programme in Rome. They were far from perfect of course. Sometimes they quarrelled and fell out. In fact, they were just like us – with failings, weaknesses and strengths.

Those early Christians were 'counter-cultural'. To a world which prized brute strength and exploitation, they offered love and service. Their way of life puzzled the cruel Roman Empire. Eventually, their love triumphed. And so they handed on the torch of faith, and the Jesus movement grew. Fast.

Churches without edges

The same is true for us. Before we can pass on the good news, we must *live* the good news – by responding to each day with gratitude and generosity. In my experience, good old-fashioned kindness, courtesy and cheerfulness go a long way. I love to be on the receiving end of such qualities, which add up to 'grace'.

If the church on the corner is to communicate good news, it must first *be* good news. This may be a straightforward matter of sharing premises – for everything from Mums & Toddlers and lunch clubs to keep-fit groups, coffee mornings and concerts. It will certainly mean working ecumenically with other churches. Increasingly, it's likely to mean working with other faith groups.

The people who gather at my local church most weeks (Sundays and weekdays) are a mixed bunch. This includes their attitude to the Christian faith. Some are convinced and committed; others are just looking – testing the water.

Some come for the sake of their children. All are welcome as we worship together, drink coffee together – and even play football together (thanks to a large vicarage garden and a large-hearted vicarage family!). We are a pretty ordinary church with a small building but good community facilities (two halls). The unorthodox 'household arrangements' of some of our members would have shocked earlier generations. But as far as I know, no one feels 'judged'. We aspire to be open and welcoming – a church without edges, which wants to share its good things.

A global perspective

A few years ago I preached at a Methodist church and met its young minister. He was a black Kenyan in England on an exchange, and was rather depressed. In Kenya he was a pioneer – a church planter. He would build up a strong church; then move on to do the same somewhere else. In Britain he had seen little obvious 'fruit' for his labours. He felt that his ministry over here was a failure.

It was a salutary reminder that much of the world is very different from Britain. The Church has taken root in surprising places. In modern China, for example, growth is very rapid – as it is in some other Asian countries, as well as in Africa and the Americas. Sociologists talk of 'the European exception'. It may not feel like it, but we belong to a fast-growing Church. And as the World Church grows, it gets ever more youthful. A typical British Christian may be elderly and affluent. A typical world Christian is young, poor and Pentecostal.

These too, are our brothers and sisters in Christ. They have much to teach us. And in a world of rapid communication, we have much that we can share with them.

Imagination and hospitality

These are two key words in 'Fresh Expressions' – an important development as we seek to hand on the torch of faith in Britain. It is enthusiastically encouraged by Archbishop Rowan Williams and has been embraced by many denominations. I had the privilege of talking to the Archbishop about this and he was keen to point out that 'Fresh Expressions' is *not* a threat to traditional styles of worship. This is what he said:

It's simply recognising that the conventional forms of worship and Christian life – going to church on Sunday mornings and so on – are wonderful, but they don't answer all the questions. Lots of people don't start there. So, how do you get to where people are, and start where they are? And that may mean stepping out of the Sunday morning routine, looking for other places, other ways of assembling people around the presence of Jesus. It can be a group of youngsters on a Friday night, it can be a young mothers' group on a Wednesday morning, it can be – and I've seen some of these extraordinary experiments – a *regular meeting for skateboarders. It can be a meeting in a country church for an hour of silence once a fortnight. So, going where people are, that's the heart of it... It's having the generosity to say, 'Well, there's more than one way of expressing what God has done for us.'* *

'Fresh Expressions' isn't just for a few super-churches. It is a mindset based on the old Christian virtue of hospitality – making other people feel welcome. This mindset frames simple but searching questions. How can we be truly hospitable? How can we take the torch of faith beyond the church to where others feel at home? How can we offer people in our locality something which they might find interesting, or even intriguing?

Moving out

From the beginning, Christians have not stayed in their comfort zone. The Church has always engaged with society and its many problems.

One recent example is 'Street Pastors' (or 'Street Angels'). Started by the black Pentecostal pastor Les Isaacs in 2003, it has been taken up in many of our towns and cities, and by many different churches working together. Interviewed on *Saturday Live* on BBC Radio 4, Les explained the simple concept. A group of Christians pray, then go into the city centre on the busiest binge-drinking nights. They are armed with drinking water, flip-flops and practical concern.

All over Britain the movement has won plaudits from police and other authorities. Street Pastors are winning respect and honour for the Church, out there in the public arena, *today* (see box on p. 14). Please pray for them.

A word for the weary

Some small struggling congregations need all their energy simply to keep the doors open and the roof from leaking. I certainly don't want to add to their burdens with extra tasks or a sense of unproductive guilt. Those who feel these pressures could do no better than to read Matthew 11.28-29 – a gentle word of comfort to the weary. What matters is that we listen to, and heed, the Lord's word to *us*. For some believers, in some situations, it isn't 'Go' but 'Come'. 'Come unto me', says Jesus, 'all who are weary and heavy-laden and I will give you rest.'

Making it local

We'll let the great missionary Bishop Lesslie Newbigin have the last word (p. 24). In Britain in the mid 1980s, after many years abroad, he encountered for the first time what he termed 'cold contempt for the Gospel'. He knew that handing on the torch of faith in our secular and superstitious society isn't easy. He also understood the importance of community, and the centrality of the old – and great – Christian virtues: faith, hope and love.

* *Rowan Revealed* CD www.yorkcourses.co.uk

QUESTIONS FOR GROUPS

BIBLE READING: Philippians 2.1-11

1. Who handed on the torch of faith to you? When, and how, did they do this?

2. Many adult Christians have dipped in and out of church at various stages in their lives. Share experiences. If this is your personal experience, why and when did it happen?

3. Re-read the section 'Learning from the Bible' (p. 21). How do you and your church measure up? It's easy for any group, including a church, to be turned in on itself – so focused on established friendships that we neglect visitors. Score yourself and your church on a welcome chart: 1 for poor, 6 for excellent. Where are you on the chart and how can you improve?

4. Most churches welcome all-comers without comment, whatever their lifestyle or domestic arrangements. Are we too relaxed? What about Christian standards? How do you feel about the fact that Prince Charles, the future head of the Church of England, was divorced, and that he re-married a divorcee in a civil ceremony, followed by a service of blessing?

5. Re-read Archbishop Rowan's quotation (p. 22). 'Fresh Expressions' is a mindset which asks, 'How can we offer appropriate and imaginative hospitality to those who do not belong to the Church?' How might your church do this more effectively in your locality?

6. Read Matthew 11.28 and then re-read the paragraph 'A word for the weary' (p. 23). Is this a word to you personally – or to your church perhaps? Discuss the Bible verse and the paragraph. Perhaps read the hymn, 'I heard the voice of Jesus say ...'

7. 'Sometimes they quarrelled and fell out' (p. 21). Re-read Philippians 2.2-3. This great New Testament passage was written precisely because two members of the church could not agree. Have you needed – do you need – to work at harmony and reconciliation within your fellowship?

8. In your view, what are the main obstacles preventing individual Christians and the churches from passing on the torch of faith? What presents us with fruitful opportunities? What gives you most encouragement?

9. Neither Rachel nor Clifford think that numbers attending church is a crucial sign of its health (tracks 53 & 54 on CD). Do you think church growth or health is mainly about numbers?

10. As this course comes to an end, you might want to plan ahead as a discussion group, a church or a group of churches.

11. Read Matthew 28.16-20 and Lesslie Newbigin's words (below). Sit quietly, then say the Lord's Prayer together.

'How can this strange story of God made man, of a crucified saviour, of resurrection and new creation become credible for those whose entire mental training has conditioned them to believe that the real world is the world which can be satisfactorily explained and managed without the hypothesis of God? I know of only one clue to the answering of that question ... a congregation which believes it.'

Bishop Lesslie Newbigin

- *York Courses* are designed for groups and individuals. They consist of a course booklet, CD or audiotape, and transcript. The CDs/audiotapes feature distinguished contributors from a wide range of churches and traditions. This makes the material ideal for ecumenical use. Many groups use the material during Lent, but the courses can be used at any time of year.

- Details of our courses and publications are listed in the centre pages of this booklet. Fuller details of our range, including the latest special offers and discounts, are available at www.yorkcourses.co.uk where you can order securely online.

- To enable each group member to have their own personal copy of this booklet, the price is reduced either when multiple copies are ordered or if you order online at www.yorkcourses.co.uk

---

Our participants are well placed to shed light on challenging contemporary issues from a Christian perspective. I wish you every blessing as you gather around this stimulating material. I hope it may support an ever more confident Christian engagement within the local community in your part of the world.

*Dr David Hope
Archbishop of York
1995-2005*

DETAILS OF PARTICIPANTS

on the CD/audiotape may be found on the inside of the back cover of this booklet.

OUR WARM THANKS to Mark Comer of *The Max Design & Print co.* for his invaluable help and expertise. Thanks also to Yolande Clarke and Linda Norman for proof-reading; to Katrina Lamb who prepared the Transcript; and to *Media Mill* for recording and producing the audio material.

Front cover image: Copyright imagedepotpro at www.iStockphoto.com

Designed and printed by The Max Design & Print co. York

THE COURSE TRANSCRIPT provides a complete record of the 'conversation' between the presenter and participants on the CD/audiotape. In an easy-to-follow format, the transcript booklet cross-references with the track numbers on the CD – making it simple to find the start of each new question posed to the participants. The transcript is especially useful for group leaders as they prepare. It can also help group members feel more confident about joining in the discussion – and enables them to go over the recorded material at leisure.

Handing on the Torch

Sacred words for a secular world

A course in five sessions written by John Young

Accompanying CD/audiotape and transcript available

YORK COURSES